Rent-A-Kid

How to start
your own business!

Larry Adler and C. Lee Crawford

Cover by
Terence Kanhai

D1115133

Scholastic Canada Ltd.

Scholastic Canada Ltd.
123 Newkirk Road, Richmond Hill, Ontario, Canada L4C 3G5

Scholastic Inc.
730 Broadway, New York, NY 10003, USA

Ashton Scholastic Pty Limited
PO Box 579, Gosford, NSW 2250, Australia

Ashton Scholastic Limited
Private Bag 1, Penrose, Auckland, New Zealand

Scholastic Publications Ltd.
Villiers House, Clarendon Avenue, Leamington Spa,
Warwickshire CV32 5PR, UK

Rent-A-Kid and Corporate Kids are trademarks of Adler Development Corporation, 785-F Rockville Pike, Suite 502, Rockville, MD 20852 U.S.A.

The authors of this book do not purport to be legal or financial experts, and legal and financial advice are beyond the scope of this book. If you need this type of advice, consult an expert.

Cover photo by Juanita Sarju

Canadian Cataloguing in Publication Data

Adler, Larry, 1973-
   Rent-a-kid

ISBN 0-590-73644-2

1. Success in business - Juvenile literature.
2. Money-making projects for children - Juvenile
literature. 3. Self-employed - juvenile literature.
I. Crawford, C. Lee. II. Title.

HF5386.A35 1992   j650.1'2   C91-095549-2

10 9 8 7 6 5 4 3 2 1   Printed in Canada   2 3 4 5 6/9
Manufactured by Webcom

Contents

Introduction

Dear Reader,

So you want to make a lot of money? Well, this is definitely the book to read. Let me share some of my tips with you.

Many people in our society believe that you have to be an adult to run a business, but you don't. Just look at me! I started my first business when I was nine years old because I wanted to be rich and famous and retire when I was twenty-one. I've been running my own business for the past eight years and I'm just seventeen. I found out that just dreaming won't get you anywhere. You have to set a goal and work for it. My first piece of advice: just get out and do it. Make some money!

How did I get going? I started out small. First,

I mowed lawns. Then I took on more handy work and eventually sold products. I went on to do product promotions, and soon I was making television appearances and had speaking engagements. Even though people said it's not a kid's place to run a business, I did it. I did it with very little help and even though I had a lot of obstacles to overcome. I did it because I had a dream and motivation.

Now, eight years later, my new goal is to convince you that YOU CAN DO IT TOO!

Larry Adler
Potomac, Maryland
1991

Rent-A-Kid

Let Us Work for You!

**Lawn Mowing • Gardening
Odd Jobs...and more!**

**Fast and Reliable
GREAT RATES**

Call Larry at 555-5555

1

How Mowing a Lawn Turned into $2000 in One Summer

When I was nine years old, I wanted to earn some extra spending money for the movies and pizza. I was too young to get a regular job and I knew I didn't want to work for someone else. When you work for someone else, you have to take what they want to pay you and work when they want you to work. I wanted to make my own decisions. I wanted to be my own boss. I wanted to run my own business.

But the only things I knew about a business were the things I'd picked up running my own lemonade stand when I was four. I sold cookies to go with the lemonade and actually made a little bit of money. Even at that age, I figured out that you have to give customers something extra if you want them to buy from you.

I knew that there's always something a little different you can do to make extra money, if you keep your eyes peeled. But now that I was nine, I wanted to make more than just nickels and dimes. I wanted to make some real money. I decided to start my own business because I wanted to be able to keep all the profits.

I looked around and figured any kid could mow lawns or wash cars without too much hassle. I knew there were lots of people in my neighborhood who would pay me to do odd jobs — if they knew I wanted to do them. I had to let them know I was for hire.

First I thought of a name for my business. I called it "Rent-A-Kid" because I was going to rent myself out to do odd jobs. Since we always got fliers in the mail trying to sell something, I figured it was a good way for me to tell people about my business. I made up a flier saying I was willing to do odd jobs, and I put a drawing on it of a kid with a rake and a hose. I borrowed nineteen dollars from my step-father to get the fliers printed. One of my friends and I passed them out around the neighborhood. We hit probably 250 townhouses within a twenty-block area around my house.

By the end of the first week, I had eight customers who wanted me to do jobs such as mowing lawns, shining shoes and washing cars. I borrowed our family's old lawn mower and started to work. The mower kept breaking down, and I had to fix it after just about every lawn. But I kept going and at the end of the week I saw my first reward money. Then I made more and more money and bought myself a gas mower to make the job easier. As the days went by, my bank account grew.

More and more calls came in and I thought up more things I could do for money — things I hadn't thought of before — like baby-sitting and cleaning out garages. My mom had given me a magician's kit when I turned seven, so now I even learned to do some simple magic tricks. I knew that parents always want magicians or clowns for kids' parties.

I had something to do almost every day all summer long. By the end of my second week in business, I had paid back the nineteen dollars I had borrowed. By the end of the summer, I had earned more than two thousand dollars! Within four years, I had built up a small-job empire. I craved success and worked toward my goal nonstop. In a way, my business was my life. At the least, it was my extracurricular activity.

I really liked earning money. Having my own

business was fun most of the time. Instead of quitting when summer was over, I decided to keep it up. Rather than spend all my money, I put it back into my business to keep it going. I got new fliers printed up telling people about all my new services, and I bought more supplies for jobs like shining shoes. Now that I was back at school, I only worked a few days after school and part of the weekend. Because I was determined, I managed to keep my grades up and make time to hang out with my friends — and still make money!

The lawn mowing jobs turned into leaf raking jobs in the autumn and then snow shoveling jobs in the winter. I still worked as the entertainment at parties and had my shoe-shining business.

By the start of the next summer, I realized I would make more money if I spent my time getting more customers and letting my friends do more of the yard work. All day long, I knocked on people's doors and convinced them to let Rent-A-Kid mow their lawns or wash their cars for them. I provided the lawn mowers and gas and sent my friends to my customers to do the work when I couldn't do it myself. Some of my friends only wanted to have jobs once in a while, so it worked out okay for them. I got the customers, and I made sure the work got done, either by my friends or by me.

I always checked the work to make sure it was done right before I collected money from the customer and paid my friends. It's important to do a job right the first time. That's why customers keep hiring you. If you do sloppy work they won't hire you again, and they may not pay you for what you've done.

When friends did a job for me, they got 60 percent of the fee. We figured it was fair that I got 40 percent because I found the customers, I supplied the equipment, such as mowers, shovels and cleaning supplies, and I was the one who had to make sure the work got done if my friends wanted to goof off that day.

I kept the business going that way through the next winter, mainly with snow shoveling jobs. I still did the clown and magician work myself, though.

By the summer I was twelve, Rent-A-Kid was pretty well-known because of the fliers I kept sending around. People also heard about me from their neighbors. I had lots of offers of work, but I couldn't do all the work myself, keep up my grades, and have time to hang out with my friends. I had to change the way I was doing business and make it into more of a company. I decided to try to expand my business even more and spend most of my time getting new customers and supervising the kids I hired.

To get more business, I'd go into a neighborhood and pass out fliers. Then later, I'd go door-to-door, asking the homeowners if they'd read the flier and offering to mow lawns for a slightly lower fee than the going rate. I made sure the work was done well, and I'd add a little extra service — like edging the lawns. I also offered to do other gardening services, like trimming hedges, and I charged a bit more for these types of jobs to make up for the lower price on the lawn. But my customers got a whole gardening package for a good price if they wanted to use Rent-A-Kid. I also got some of them to hire me to do other odd jobs. After I'd convinced my customers that Rent-A-Kid's work was superior, I slowly raised my prices.

I hired a couple of kids in the neighborhood to work regularly. We agreed that I would pay them a certain amount for the job, and I would pay them at the end of each day, after I'd checked their work.

Each morning, I'd send them to a certain neighborhood and get them to do all my customers in that area. They did housecleaning, pet care, plant care and fence painting, as well as yard work. I got walkie-talkies and my employees would call in to me every hour to see if there were any new jobs to add to their lists, or if they needed help with a problem.

The business kept getting bigger and I just couldn't handle all the work. I needed to hire more kids to work with me. I advertised in the local newspaper for kids aged fourteen to seventeen who wanted to work for me and get paid by the hour. About 100 kids called.

I hired a couple of older kids with cars to act as supervisors and to drive the younger ones and the necessary equipment to the different neighborhoods. By this time I had as many as twenty kids working for me, and I had customers in lots of neighborhoods beyond my own. I paid the older kids with cars eight dollars an hour and I paid the younger ones five dollars an hour.

I'd ride my bike around the different neighborhoods to check on how the kids were doing and to collect the money from my customers. Then I'd stop at the kids' places and give them their share. When winter came, I had some of the kids work for my customers again on weekends.

I had learned a lot, especially the summer I was trying to expand. I found out business can get complicated. For instance, when some of my customers needed carpentry or plumbing work or wanted carpets installed, I took it on. I hired adults to do the work. But it turned out to be more trouble than it was worth because the work is complicated. You have to have insurance in case anything goes wrong. Sometimes you have to pay a deposit to professionals in advance, and if they charge too much, you can't get the customer to pay you enough to make a profit on the job. It gets too complicated.

I also took on window washing jobs, but I soon saw that it could be dangerous for kids to work on ladders — and you have to have insurance in case they have an accident. I figured out that it was better to take on jobs that weren't too risky or, if I did take them on, to do the risky jobs myself.

That winter I realized I needed to do something new. Rent-A-Kid was pretty easy to run now that I'd been doing it for more than three years. I had regular customers, I had a lot of kids working for me — kids that I could count on — and I was making good money!

I figured Rent-A-Kid was a success, and now it was time to move on and teach other kids how to do the same thing. I also wanted to branch out and start another kind of business — to take on new challenges.

2

How One Business Turned into Four Businesses Overnight

The winter I turned twelve, my family went to Florida to visit my aunt, who owned a store. I found two huge boxes of plastic baskets stored in her basement and asked her if I could buy them from her. She said okay, and I took them back home when we left.

My aunt had used some of the baskets to display gifts in her store, and I figured that I could make some money if I made up gift baskets and sold them to gift stores and to the neighbors for special occasions.

The baskets were wrapped flat and had to be put

together, so I hired some kids to assemble them. I paid them by the basket. They could assemble the baskets at my place, or take them home and assemble them and bring them back. Once some baskets were assembled, I bought things to put in them — like chocolate hearts, stuffed animals, and cards for Valentine's Day, candy canes and toys for Christmas, and candies, favors and balloons for birthdays — and took some sample baskets to gift stores in the mall near my home. I called myself "Basket Boy."

The store owners would give me orders for different kinds of baskets, and I'd make them up and deliver them. I had to decide on a price, so I figured out what it cost me to make them and then doubled that cost so I could make a nice profit. I also got lots of orders from making up Basket Boy fliers and passing them around the neighborhood.

When I was looking for things to put in the baskets, I talked to a lot of different companies that sold party favors and things like that. Because of Basket Boy, I was finding out about many manufacturers' products and was making contacts in the gift stores. Within a few weeks, I had another business idea: perhaps some of these manufacturers might pay me to be their sales representative in my area.

My mom had a business selling products from our basement when I was younger, so I knew how it worked. I'd convince stores to sell the products I represented and the people who made the product would pay me to do it. After all, who knows better than a kid what products a kid wants to buy?

Many of the companies thought I was too young to be a sales representative. But I kept after them. I asked them to give me a try for one month based on my experience making Rent-A-Kid work. Lots of them said okay, and I started my third company — Larry Adler and Associates. I became the youngest sales rep in North America.

Acting as a sales rep was challenging and fun. I kept asking more and more companies if I could represent them. By the end of that year, I was representing more than two dozen companies. They made all kinds of different products.

I decided to represent only stuff that would appeal to kids and teenagers.

I specialized so that I wouldn't spread myself too thin. Store buyers began to listen to me because they knew any product I asked them to sell in their stores was a product my friends and I would like to buy. I went to trade shows and conventions where manufacturers bring the products they want to sell and store buyers look and decide if they want to buy the products to sell in their stores.

I became known at some trade shows as "The Kid Rep." At these shows, I realized people would pay me for my opinions about whether or not a kid would like to buy their product. People started sending me new kids' products and asking me my opinion of them, and a couple of companies paid me to promote their products by going on radio and television and talking about how good they were. I decided to become a consultant to people who wanted to sell things to kids, so I formed my fourth company, "KIDCORP."

Soon I was getting calls from all over the country from people with new products. I did promotions for all kinds of companies, national and international.

Mostly I charged by the hour. I charged kids half what I charged adults. But sometimes people who wanted me to give my opinion on a product or promote a product didn't have a lot of money to spend. If I figured it was a good product, I'd make another kind of deal. I'd promote it free at first, so I could have another success on my resume. Others agreed to pay for my plane tickets or hotel room if I went to a trade show and helped them promote their products.

In the five years I'd been working, I'd made far more money than I'd ever dreamed I could make —

and I was only working at it part time. It was time to make a change.

The more money I made and the more media attention I got, the more I was spurred on. As people got to know my name, I was written about in newspapers and then asked to discuss my business ideas on talk shows. As the public grew to know me, I was asked to speak to groups of kids like myself and tell them how I started my own businesses.

I still keep plowing any money I make back into the businesses to make them grow. I want financial success by the time I'm twenty-one. I want to have enough money so I can retire and not worry about money any more. Then I'm going to work and make money just for the fun of it!

Rent-A-Kid has always been my favorite project, probably because it was my first and it worked out so well. Today, I'm working to help kids all over do what I have done. Because newspaper and television reporters have done stories about my success with Rent-A-Kid, my first business has made me well-known even in places outside my home in Washington. I've had thousands of calls and letters from kids all over Canada and the U.S. — from kids who have big plans and great ideas and want some help in setting up their own businesses. I've found out that too many kids believe what adults and other kids tell them — that they're too young to succeed in business and their plans are just silly kid dreams. It's not what I believe.

I think that money is money no matter how old you are, and if you have an idea to make money then you should go ahead and try it out. Young or old, whether you work ten hours a day or ten hours a week, I consider anyone who owns a business to be an entrepreneur.

Any kid can start his or her own business. That's why I wrote this book. It'll help you get going in business, just like I got going with Rent-A-Kid. If you just want to make a little spending money, you can run your own car wash or yard sale every few months. If you want more money, you can do lawns or baby-sit for regular customers, or you can turn a hobby, such as baking, into cash.

There are several secrets to my success, and they're included in the following chapters along with suggestions for starting your own business. The two most important tips, though, are to work hard and take advantage of opportunities. You can't be lazy and expect to make any money. And you always have to keep your eyes open for new ways to advertise your name or promote your business.

My story is proof that kids can accomplish whatever they set their minds to!

3
Setting Realistic Goals

Deciding what goal you want to reach is a big part of any business. You have to figure out what you want before you can make a plan to go after it. What is your goal? Is it extra pocket money for the movies, a new bicycle, money for university tuition? Or perhaps you want to be a millionaire by the time you're twenty-one?

All these goals are possible to achieve. What adults may call fantasies or dreams, I consider realistic goals. You just have to start out small and plan well.

Think of yourself as creating a circle that is growing bigger and bigger. You start out small at the center. As you grow and you get older, the circle expands all around you. Make sure you keep yourself open to growth in every direction.

If you narrow your focus to one direction or you stop growing, the circle shrinks.

Don't just keep your eyes looking ahead in a narrow, straight line. Things are going on around you in every direction. As you grow, you accomplish your small goals and set new and bigger ones for yourself. Your goals should keep changing as you change.

So you want to make a million dollars by next Tuesday?

To help you figure out what it is you want to achieve, write down your answers to these questions — and be specific:

- What do I want to be when I get older?
- What do I want to achieve in life?
- How much money do I want to make?
- By when do I want to make it?
- Are these goals realistic?

Deciding you want to make a million dollars by Tuesday is not realistic, but it may not be impossible to make a million dollars by the time you're ready for college. However, a more realistic goal may be to make two thousand dollars by the end of the summer or by Christmas vacation. You have to start out small, but don't be held back by other people's negative opinions. Listen to yourself and your feelings when other people tell you something can't be done. Who ever thought a pet rock would sell, for instance? Or what about tins of West Coast air, pieces of the moon, or bags of ice cubes at gas stations? It's all in the way you think about the product and how you promote or market it. You have to believe in your product and yourself.

When I first started Rent-A-Kid, I was looking for extra spending money so I borrowed the family mower and began cutting a few lawns. My goal was to make enough money to be able to buy extra candy and more clothes and go to more movies. I said to myself, "I made ten dollars today, so I can make fifteen dollars tomorrow." The next day I made the fifteen dollars — and I raised my goal a little higher. Using a chart like the one on the next page will help you get started. Make one up for yourself and use it as motivation. Some days you may make less than you planned, other days more. But don't give up. Keep going, because over time you can reach your goals.

Look at the chart. What's the total amount of money you made? Seventy-four dollars. That's

DATE	JOB	MONEY
7/1/9-	lawn mowing	$8.00
7/2/9-	lawn mowing	$9.00
	baby-sitting	$4.00
7/4/9-	plant bushes	$15.00
7/5/9-	wax car	$10.00
	cleaning house	$20.00
7/6/9-	selling own	
	baking	$8.00

seventy-four dollars you didn't have at the beginning of the week. Even if you have to pay your parents back four dollars for the lawn mower gas or baking supplies, you're still seventy dollars ahead.

But what's so great about starting your own business, anyway?

Well, by the time you're fifteen, the labor laws in most places will allow you to work for someone else, like a fast-food place or a gas station. But anyone who hires you will probably pay you the minimum wage — that's the lowest amount of money the law allows them to pay — for every hour you work. They will also pretty much tell you what hours they want you to work.

If you start your own business and you're a hard worker, you can make more money than you might make working for someone else. This is especially true if you give customers a little extra for their money, because you can charge more for your time than the hourly minimum wage.

Running your own business also means you can work as many hours as you like and you can make up your own schedule. You can work only after school two days a week or only on Saturday mornings — if that's what you want. You just have to go out and find the jobs in your neighborhood that fit your schedule.

Getting started

After you've set a goal, the next thing you have to do is decide what kind of business you want to start. Talking with a friend or relative you trust can help create ideas. Don't discuss your ideas with someone who will put you down or laugh at you. Talk with someone who wants to see you get ahead and will help you figure out ways to get around problems.

It helps to ask yourself what you can do already that will make you some money. I already knew how to do simple magic tricks because I got a magician's kit when I was seven years old. So I started getting myself hired out for kids' birthday parties. It was easy to go from being a magician to being a clown. I got my sister's old Halloween costume, got hired for parties, and started doing what I'd seen clowns do. I'd charge ten dollars for a half-hour show.

Think about what kind of talents you have that you can use. Are you good at making paper kites? Why not see if you can sell them by putting an ad in your local paper or going to a toy store?

Are you good at looking after your younger brothers or sisters? Why not get a job as a parent's helper or a baby-sitter after school or on weekends?

Are you good at cooking? Why not ask friends or neighbors who work full-time if they want to hire you to get dinner ready for them a couple of times every week?

Also ask yourself what you can learn to do that will make you money. I'd never mowed a lawn in my life, but I figured I could learn. So I just watched my older brother David mow our lawn. I saw the pattern he went in, and I learned to do it myself.

Get a friend or relative to teach you to embroider things that you can sell. Learn to put together model airplanes or kites, paint them with wild colors, and sell them to gift stores. Get someone with a green thumb to teach you what you need to know about gardening, and start your own gardening business.

If you want to learn how to do something and you have nobody to teach you, go to the library and get a book about it. Then just practice until you get good at it. *Remember: you don't have to be perfect. After all, you're just starting out. Practice makes perfect!* You can charge a little less while you're learning. When you become really good at it you can raise your prices.

Setting your price

Once you've decided what you can do to make money, you have to decide how much you can charge for what you do. Ask a parent or teacher to help you find out what the legal minimum wage is in your state or province. For example, if it's four dollars an hour, try to at least double this rate. You should usually charge at least one hour's pay for a job that takes less than an hour, or it isn't worth doing. Your minimum pay per job — even if the job takes less than an hour — should almost always be eight dollars.

When I started out, I mowed the lawns of townhouses around my place. I could finish most of the yards in about fifteen or twenty minutes. But I still charged five dollars for the full hour. In other words, I charged five dollars an hour or five dollars per job. But since I could do as many as three lawns in an hour, I was sometimes able to make fifteen dollars an hour.

1 job in 1 hour	= $5 per hour
1 job in 1/2 hour	= $5 per half-hour
2 half hour jobs x $5	= $10 per hour
1 job in 20 minutes	= $5 per 20 minutes
3 20-minute jobs x $5	= $15 per hour

When you're doing jobs like just running errands, you may want to charge by the half-hour or less. There aren't many people who'll pay you five dollars just to run to the corner to buy a loaf of bread or mail a letter. In those cases, you'll want to charge a minimum of about two dollars per job, depending on how long it takes you.

There are other things to think about when you're selling products. If you're painting custom T-shirts or making kites, you have to figure in the cost of the materials you need to make them. For a T-shirt, take the cost of the plain shirt, paints, and anything else you use. If you're selling to a store, figure out what anywhere from fifteen to thirty percent of that cost is, and add it to the total cost of the materials. The amount that you add to the cost of your materials is called the "mark-up." The stores then turn around and add a mark-up or percentage on top of that when they sell it. That's how they make a profit.

If you're selling directly to the public, such as by advertising with fliers and going door-to-door, you can add fifty per cent to the cost of your materials and charge the same as a store would.

> **TIP:** Sell products door-to-door around holidays. For instance, sell candy right before Halloween, when people need it.

First, you should figure out what your time is worth. Here's a way to figure it out:

- Find out what the minimum wage is in your area. *You should always set your hourly rate higher than this amount. You're worth it!*
- Add 50% on to the minimum wage. For example, if minimum wage is $4.00 per hour, add $2.00 to get an hourly rate of $6.00. This is usually the *least* you should charge. And remember, you can always raise your rate as you get more experience.
- Your rate will also depend on the usual rate in your area. Ask around and find out what other people are charging per hour for similar services before you decide.

A pricing example: custom T-shirts

Once you know what you are planning to charge per hour for your time, you have to figure out how long it takes you to make each item.

Then, add together the cost of all the materials you use to make your T-shirt.

The cost of materials, the mark-up on the materials and the cost of your time added together should be your cost per item, or the price you charge the customer.

Cost of material for 1 T-shirt   = \$2.50

50% mark-up on \$2.50   = \$1.25

Amount of time to make 1 T-shirt

    = 1 hour (at \$6/hour)   = \$6.00

Total cost of 1 custom T-shirt:

    = (\$2.50 + \$1.25 + \$6.00)   = \$9.75

These are just examples of how to do the calculations. Check out what the usual rate for your product or service is in your area. Your price should be close to that. Ask an adult who knows about these things to help you figure out what realistic prices are for your business. Then do the calculations and write down the final prices. This will be your price list which you will show customers who want to know what your products or services cost.

Choosing the right business for you

There are three basic areas to look at when deciding to start a business. You can:

- sell services that don't require any special equipment, for example baby-sitting.
- sell services and provide any necessary equipment, for example gardening.
- sell products, for example lemonade at a lemonade stand, or homemade crafts.

The next two chapters give you a whole bunch of ideas for businesses you can start that sell your services and the chapter after that gives you ideas for selling products you make. These three chapters will also tell you about the kinds of things you need to know to get started in a business, such as:

- where to look for customers
- what questions to ask
- how to figure out a price or wage
- what kind of equipment you may need to start out
- special tips on how to sell your service or product.

Some businesses are going to cost you some money to get started. You may need a bicycle, car wax, gardening tools or hobby supplies. You'll also have to get some fliers printed to advertise your services.

I borrowed the family lawn mower when I started my first business. It was kind of old and kept breaking down. I decided I needed a lawn mower of my own because I was wasting valuable time trying to make the old one go again. After I made some money, I bought a new mower so I could do more lawns in less time.

If you don't have the right tools or someone who can lend you a few dollars to get going, don't be discouraged. You can start out with jobs that don't require any money up front — like running errands, baby-sitting or tutoring — until you have enough saved up to buy what you need to start another kind of business. Start small and grow!

Or, if your parents give you a weekly allowance, save up what you need out of that. It may take you a little longer, but you'll get there. Put your money in a savings account — not only will you be less tempted to spend it, but you'll earn interest and your savings will grow.

If none of the jobs in this book are exactly right for you, they will at least get you thinking about a good business idea. Use them to come up with an idea for a new kind of business that's all your own.

Every business should be a safe business

It's very important that you make sure the business you choose is a safe kind of business for a kid to be in. The ideas I put in this book are mainly for jobs that don't require you to go inside the homes of strangers. When you're selling door-to-door or collecting money, make sure you stay outside on the step, even if it's cold. If they say they won't pay you unless you come inside, go and get one of your parents to go to the home with you. Never go inside the home of anyone you don't know. Even if you do know the people, don't go inside if they make you feel uneasy or uncomfortable in any way. Just say you'd rather stand outside.

If you're going to baby-sit, be a parent's helper or clean house, only do it for people you or your parents know. If anyone in the house you're working at does anything to make you feel uncomfortable, *leave and tell your parents*.

If a stranger wants to hire you to do a job that's inside his or her home, take one of your parents with you to discuss the job first. If your parent has checked out the customer and you feel comfortable with the customer too, you can go ahead and do the work.

Remember, never stay in any situation if you feel afraid or uncomfortable. Leave and tell an adult about it at once!

4

Putting Your Services on the Market

This chapter is full of ideas for businesses you can start that sell your services — without any special equipment. You're selling your own "brains and brawn" — your intelligence and your ability to work hard.

You need little or no money to start up in a business that requires no equipment, but as you make some cash, you may want to buy things that will help you do the job faster, more easily or more efficiently. Or you may want to spend some of the profits on promotion ideas to expand your business and make it grow. Either way, there's money to be made — *if* you're willing to do the work.

Baby-sitting

This can involve looking after people's children while the parents are out, taking younger kids to dentist or doctor appointments after school and walking younger kids to and from school.

In all cases, you'll be responsible for keeping the children safe.

How to start:

Put up notices in religious centers, schools, community centers and local stores. Tell all your family's friends and relatives that you're available and ask them to tell their friends about you.

Cost to you:

None.

How to price:

Find out what the going rate is for baby-sitting in your area and then add fifty cents an hour to your fee. You can justify this by advertising that you play with the kids instead of just putting them in front of the television set and, because you want to keep all your attention on the children, you never have your friends over when you baby-sit. People will pay for quality work!

Charge one dollar more than your hourly rate for each hour you baby-sit past midnight.

Figure out a flat rate for weekend and overnight sitting jobs.

If your customers' homes are too far for you to reach on foot, make sure your customers drive you to and from your home or pay for a cab to take you.

If you have enough room and your parents say it's okay, you can baby-sit kids in your home. Tell your customers you charge less if they drop the kids off and pick them up at your place.

Tips:

$ Always make sure your parents know the name of your baby-sitting customer and their address and phone number.

$ Make up a list of things you need to know, and go over the list with your customers before they leave.

$ To make sure your friends don't drop in on you, don't tell them where you'll be.

$ Collect books and toys for kids, and take them with you when you baby-sit. The kids will look forward to seeing what you've brought.

BABY-SITTING INFORMATION

Customer's name: _____

Address: _____

Phone number: _____

Phone where customers can be
reached: _____

Neighbor's phone number: _____

Emergency numbers:

Ambulance: _____

Police: _____

Fire department: _____

Doctor: _____

Name of any medicine the
children need to take and
instructions for giving it: _____

_____

_____

Children's allergies or
special problems: _____

_____

_____

Parent's helper

You'll give a parent with small kids a hand. You'll make meals for the kids and look after them. You may make easy-to-cook meals for the family and do some light house cleaning.

How to start:

Ask friends, relatives and neighbors if they need you to help them with their kids.

Pass out fliers saying you're available and responsible. Ask friends of your family if they will give you a good reference. If they will, advertise on your flier that you have references. List the work that you are willing to do.

Place fliers in local stores and community centers.

Place an ad in your neighborhood paper.

Cost to you:

It will cost money to have fliers printed up.

You may have to pay to put an ad in the paper.

You may need bus fare to get to the customer.

How to price:

Charge by the hour. Find out what most people in your area charge for baby-sitting, and then add between 50 cents and a dollar per hour if you're going to be doing housework.

Tips:

> $ Collect some of your old storybooks and games to help amuse the little kids.

> $ Learn how to make simple things like macaroni and cheese, cookies or soup and sandwiches. Tell your customers the kinds of meals you're good at cooking.

Tutoring

You'll help other kids with schoolwork. Stick to subjects that you do well in yourself.

How to start:

Ask your teachers to recommend you to other students.

Go to the teachers of grades below yours and tell them you're available to tutor.

Put up fliers in local stores and your community center as well as in the school lunchroom and library.

Ask friends of the family and relatives if any of their kids need a tutor in the subjects that are your best ones.

Cost to you:

You may need to pay bus fare.

It will cost you to have fliers printed.

How to price:

Ask a teacher or your school guidance counselor what the going rate is for tutors.

Tips:

$ If you have a place in your home where you can tutor without a lot of noise or hassle, you can charge students ten percent less than your usual hourly rate if they come to you. You save traveling time and bus fare that way.

$ Use your imagination and come up with ways to make the lessons more interesting. Use drawings, flash cards, or teaching tricks to make learning fun. You might be able to get old or damaged books from your students' schools to help you.

Planning children's parties

You'll help parents plan their kids' birthday parties. You'll send invitations and arrange for food, a birthday cake, candles, decorations, party favors and entertainment. You'll set up for the party and clean up afterwards.

How to start:

Have fliers printed up to list all the services you provide.

Pass the fliers around the neighborhood and put them up at nursery schools, grade schools, day care centers, stores and malls.

Ask all your friends and relatives to keep you in mind for their parties, and ask them to mention your services to everyone they know.

How to price:

Figure out how much time it will take you to plan the party, shop for it, set it up, supervise it,

Success Story

When I was about nine years old, I planned a surprise party for my mother and it was really pretty easy. I made a list of all the things I had to do:

✓ Invitations
✓ Food
✓ Drinks
✓ Cake and candles
✓ Decorations
✓ Get Mom out of the house
✓ Clean up

The success of a party is all in the planning! I figured out what I could do myself and what I needed help with. I got the numbers of all my mother's friends from her address book and then I called and invited them. I got Mom's best friend to get her out of the house for a while and bring her back at a certain time. I ordered a cake at a local bakery and got lots of soda pop. I asked all Mom's friends to bring food.

It was a great party. Everyone had a good time. If I could organize a party when I was nine years old, you can do it too!

provide the entertainment and clean up after it. Charge your hourly rate for the time.

Figure out what it will cost for food, favors, invitations, decorations, entertainment and any other things you may need to buy, and add twenty percent. The 20 percent is your profit.

Add together your hourly rate and the cost of supplies (plus 20 percent), and tell the customer that this is your budget. Ask for the money you'll spend on supplies as a deposit before the party. After the party is over, bill the customer for your time and the 20 percent profit.

Tips:

$ Sit down and think of some fun themes for kids' parties, for example a jungle party with animal decorations and games, or a clown party with clown make-up for the kids to put on. Think of something that's fun for that age group and not too expensive. Talk to the parents about their kid's interests and have them choose a theme.

$ If you're a good photographer, volunteer to take pictures of the party and charge double what the photo developing costs are. If you have a friend with a video camera, offer to have the friend videotape the party. Charge

extra for the service, and split the video fee
with your friend.

$ If you're doing the party alone, limit the num-
ber of kids invited to about six. If there are
more, you'll have to hire a friend or relative
to help you. Don't try to run a huge party all
by yourself to save the cost of help. You'll
make a mess of it and end up with a headache.

Cleaning yards and garages

You'll be clearing everything out of a garage or
yard, sweeping, raking or hosing down the area,
putting the trash and old junk in garbage bags and
then putting everything else back neatly.

How to start

Have fliers printed up listing your services and
pass them out around the neighborhood, in stores,
community centers, malls and religious centers.

Canvass friends and relatives to see if they have
any jobs for you, and ask them to tell their friends
about your services.

Cost to you:

You will have to pay to have fliers printed up.

You may want to buy a wagon and supply the
garbage bags and cleaning supplies.

How to price:

Charge by the hour at your basic hourly rate. Charge 25 percent more if you provide cleaning supplies and garbage bags.

Tips:

$ While you're doing the cleaning, watch for things that need a bit of repairing or a coat of paint. Offer to fix them up for your hourly fee.

$ Remember to wear heavy shoes or boots and gloves to protect yourself.

Helping people move

This involves helping people pack and unpack boxes, load and unload boxes and furniture, and clean out the old dwelling and the new one. You can also take care of children or pets on moving day.

How to start:

Send out fliers advertising your moving service and list all the jobs you can do.

Put notices or fliers up on bulletin boards in apartment buildings, because people who live in apartments tend to move more often than people in houses.

Put notices or fliers up in community centers, local supermarkets and convenience stores.

Cost to you:

You will have to pay to have fliers printed.

You may also need bus fare to get to the customer.

How to price:

Charge by the hour at your basic hourly rate. If you supply boxes and newspaper, charge for the boxes, for example 40 cents for small boxes and 75 cents for large ones.

Tips:

$ If you're using your head, you'll convince your customers to let you supply packing boxes and newspapers for them to use for packing. Then go to the local supermarket and liquor store every few days and get boxes. Save them up. Also save your family's newspapers.

$ You will probably want to get a friend to help you. Keep 60 percent of your earnings, since you found the job and got the packing materials. Give your friend 40 percent.

Grocery shopping

This involves taking people's shopping lists, doing the shopping and then delivering the groceries.

How to start:

Get fliers or notices printed up and distribute them around the neighborhood.

Put up fliers in the local grocery stores, super-markets and seniors' centers.

Go to the local supermarket on a Saturday and hand out fliers to people who are shopping.

Cost to you:

You will have to pay to get fliers printed up.

You'll need a bundle buggy or wagon. Look for one around your home or borrow one from a friend or neighbor until you can save up to buy your own.

How to price:

Charge by the hour at your basic hourly rate.

Tips:

$ Make up a sample basic shopping list like the one your mom or dad uses. Break the list down into categories, leaving lots of space between items. Put your name and phone number on the bottom.

$ Have these lists printed up and pass them out with the fliers. Each time you shop for cus-tomers, leave new lists with them so they'll use them and remember to call you.

SHOPPING LIST

Customer's name: _____

Phone number: _____

Address: _____

_____

GROCERIES

Fruit: _____

Vegetables: _____

Meat: _____

Milk products: _____

Cooking supplies: _____

Bread: _____

Personal supplies: _____

Cleaning supplies: _____

Household products: _____

Deli or specialty items: _____

Other: _____

_____

_____

Your name and phone number: _____

_____

$ Collect the money for the groceries from the customer before you go shopping. Estimate how much you'll need and add 20 percent to be sure you have enough.

$ Write out a simple receipt for the money (see Chapter 7 for an example) and give it to the customer right then. Make sure you keep the cash register receipt for the shopping so you can give it to your customer and collect any extra money.

$ When you return with the groceries and the store receipt, ask the customer to return your receipt to you. That way you've got a record in case there's any misunderstanding later.

$ Make sure you have a little bit of extra cash of your own when you go shopping just in case the customer hasn't guessed the total exactly.

Taking out the trash

This service involves carrying people's garbage to the curb on garbage collection day and returning trash cans after they're emptied.

How to start:

Have fliers made up and pass them out around the neighborhood and in local grocery stores.

Find out when collection day is in different

neighborhoods and go door-to-door the night before offering to take out the trash for a fee.

Cost to you:
Other than the cost of having fliers printed up, this only takes your time and energy.

How to price:
Since it probably only takes a few minutes to take out the garbage of a home, you can charge a flat rate every week or month that works out to the minimum hourly wage. Or you can charge a flat rate for each bag of garbage.

Tips:
You're not likely to get rich just taking out the trash, so check around your customers' homes, see what other jobs they might need to have done and then ask if they want to hire you to do them.

Digging gardens and flower beds
You'll be helping people dig up their gardens to prepare them for spring or winter.

How to start:
Check out the homes in your neighborhood to see which have gardens. Go door-to-door in the

early spring and fall and offer your services.

Have fliers printed up, and pass them around the neighborhood.

Post fliers in local stores and in the plant stores and nurseries in your area.

Cost to you:

The fliers will cost money to be printed.

Borrow your family's tools, or you can probably use the customer's tools until you can make enough money to buy your own.

How to price:

Charge by the hour at your usual hourly rate. Or, if you think it will make you more money, charge by the job.

Tips:

- $ Do a good job and then offer to do other gardening or yard chores as well.
- $ Study some gardening books from the library and then make suggestions to the customer about how to make the garden look better.

Gift shopping and wrapping

You'll shop for special gifts for people who don't have time to shop, then gift wrap and deliver the gifts.

How to start:

Make up fliers listing your services and pass them around to neighbors and friends.

Go to seniors' homes and pass out fliers or ask permission to put up fliers on any notice boards.

Post notices or fliers in local stores and community centers.

Put an advertisement in the local newspaper.

How to price:

Charge by the hour at your standard rate. Don't

Success Story

One sales pitch I used a lot in my fliers and when I was going door-to-door was to ask, *"Who knows better than a kid what a kid wants? No one. A kid knows what a kid likes to eat. A kid knows what a kid likes to play with. A kid knows what a kid likes to wear."*

Another pitch I used, especially with people who seemed to be really busy all the time, was to ask, *"Isn't your time worth much more per hour than what you'd be paying me to do this job?"*

forget to charge for the time it takes you to talk with your customer about what to buy.

Add on the time it takes for shopping, wrapping, and delivery.

Charge at least five dollars to wrap a parcel, depending on the size.

Tips:

$ Prepare a standard list of things that will help you choose a gift and leave copies of it with your customers. Ask basic things about the person the gift is for, such as age and sex, favorite color, favorite music, basic interests and hobbies, tastes in clothing and toys. Also be sure to ask the price range. The answers to these questions will give you a good idea where to start.

$ Be sure to keep the receipts from your purchases in case you need to return something.

$ Holidays such as Christmas are a good time to sell this kind of service.

Planning yard sales

This involves setting up a yard sale two or three times a year. You'll advertise the sale and collect stuff from neighbors and friends to sell at it. It will be held on your front lawn or driveway.

How to start:

Get your family's permission to clean out your basement, attic, or garage to find stuff to sell.

Go door-to-door asking people if they have anything they want to sell at a yard sale.

Collect the stuff, put prices on the items and set a date for the sale.

Send out fliers to advertise the sale.

Put an ad in the local paper to advertise the sale.

Cost to you:

There will be printing costs for the fliers, and the ad will cost something as well.

The price tags for the items won't cost you anything if you make up your own.

How to price:
Tell the people who give you stuff for the sale that, because you advertised and set up the sale and collected the items, you'll keep 40 percent of what you get for their items and give them the rest.

Tips:
$ If you're selling for several people at once, color-code price tags so you can keep track of whose stuff is whose. Keep the tags from sold items so you have a record of what you sold, and for how much.

$ If you have the time, fix things that need only minor repairs, clean up things that are dirty or dusty and put paint on anything that can use a fresh coat. You'll get twice as much money for things if they are clean and they look like they work.

Office helper
You'll work for a company as a "go-fer" after school. You'll run errands, do filing, answer phones, do photocopying and stuff envelopes.

How to start:

Put the word out among family and friends that you're available to do office work after school.

Have fliers made up and pass them around to any small businesses in your area. List the things you can do and the price you charge per hour.

Try to find work in one or two places a couple of days after school each week.

Cost to you:

Printing the fliers will cost you money.

You may have to pay bus fare to get to the customer.

You may need a bicycle to run errands.

How to price:

Charge by the hour if it's not regular work. Give a flat rate if a customer gives you regular work. Start out at a little less than your usual rate to get your foot in the door and then raise your prices as your skills increase and you prove that you're reliable.

Tips:

$ Always dress neatly when you work for a company. It won't impress them if you look scruffy. Find out if there's a dress code and stick to it!

$ It's a better bet to find this kind of work with small companies than with big companies. Bigger companies see it as too much paperwork to hire kids for part-time work.

House sitting

You'll be looking after people's houses or apartments when they're away for weekends or long vacations. This can involve picking up mail, watering plants, making sure the lights are on during part of the evening, mowing grass, shoveling snow, watering the garden and making sure there are no broken pipes or other problems.

How to start:

Tell relatives, friends and neighbors that you have a house-sitting business.

Have fliers printed up listing all your services and distribute them around the neighborhood.

Post fliers or notices in locations such as local stores, community centers, religious centers and malls.

Cost to you:

You will have to pay to have fliers printed.

Depending on how far away your customers are, you may need bus fare or a bicycle.

How to price:

If there's little work, charge for one hour a day at your usual rate, even if it takes you less than an hour a day. If there's more work involved, such as mowing the lawn, charge more than minimum wage per hour for the extra work.

Tips:

$ Ask people to give you references, and mention on your flier that you provide references.

$ Keep your eyes open for other job ideas when you're at your customers' places and offer to do other work for them later.

$ Write down in detail all the things you agree to do. Always get a phone number where you can reach your customers in case there's an emergency.

Painting

You'll paint things like railings, decks, porches, garages, fences and things that don't require a lot of climbing on ladders.

How to start:

Have fliers printed up listing the kind of painting you do and pass them out around the neighborhood and at other locations such as community

centers, hardware stores and paint stores.

Canvass all your friends and relatives to see if they or any of their friends need you to work for them.

Cost to you:

Having fliers printed up will cost you some money.

You should buy your own paint brushes and scrapers.

How to price:

Charge by the hour. If you are only responsible for painting, charge a little less. If you go to the paint store, bring the paint swatches to the customer, and then buy the paint and deliver it, you should charge your usual hourly rate or a little more. Make sure you keep the receipt for the paint and give it to the customer with your bill.

Tips:

$ Good painters never leave a messy work place. Always clean up any spills and leave the area neat and tidy.

Bulk mailing

This job involves copying or printing bulk announcements or letters, addressing them, folding them and putting them in envelopes.

How to start:

Get fliers printed up advertising your services and prices and give them out in your neighborhood.

Drop off fliers at small offices and stores at the local malls.

Post fliers in community centers and religious centers.

How to price:

Offer one price for a complete mailing service which includes picking up the letter or announcement and making copies of it, putting the letters into the envelopes, making up address labels and putting them on the envelopes, putting stamps on the envelopes and mailing the envelopes.

Charge by the number of pieces of mail. Figure out how many letters you can stuff in an envelope in one hour. Divide that number by your hourly wage. Then add 25 percent more to cover the amount of time it takes to do the other parts of the job. That total is your price per piece of mail.

If your customers provide the copies, envelopes, and address labels and you won't have to spend as much time preparing the mail, give them a better price.

Tips:

$ It's best to get a deposit up front from your customers if they want you to buy things such as envelopes, stamps and labels. That way you don't have to put out any money and wait for them to pay you back for your expenses. Make sure you keep all receipts and give them to your customer with the bill.

$ If your family has a computer and you know how to use it, you can add mailing lists to your bulk mailing service, or you can just start a mailing list business by making address labels for small businesses and stores.

5

Spend a Little,
Earn a Lot!

The jobs discussed in this chapter require some
equipment. Try to borrow the things to get started.
However, if you don't know anyone with a computer,
a camera, or any of the other equipment you might
need, you'll have to invest a little money. If you don't
have enough, see if a friend or relative will let you
borrow the money if you promise to pay it back a
little each week from your earnings.

Remember, spending a little now can help you
earn a lot later!

Some of these jobs are also for older kids who
have skills such as typing.

Shoe-shining

You'll be cleaning and polishing people's shoes
and boots. You can either pick up and deliver foot-
wear around the neighborhood or you can get permission to set up at a mall.

How to start:

Have fliers made up saying what you do, and
pass them out around the neighborhood.

Ask the manager of your local mall if you can set
up outside the mall after school and on weekends.

Ask at your local shoe repair store if you can set
up in the store after school or on weekends, and
offer to pay the owner 10 percent of what you earn.

Cost to you:

You'll need a shoe-shining kit with polish,
brushes, buffers, weather protector spray, and
cleaning rags. You can start with a cardboard box,
brown and black polish, a rag and a shoe brush, and
add to your kit as you make money.

You will have to pay the cost of printing fliers.

How to price:

Here's how to decide how much to charge to shine a pair of shoes if you're working in a shop or a mall. Figure out how many pairs of shoes you can do in an hour and divide that number by your hourly rate. This is your first total.

Then add on your materials cost — probably between 50 cents and a dollar per pair of shoes. Then add the two totals together. This is your price per pair.

If you collect shoes from around the neighborhood and return them cleaned, you should add 25 percent to your price for the extra service.

Tips:

$ Charge more for polishing boots than you do for shoes.

$ Give people a deal if they have five or more pairs of shoes or boots done each week.

$ If you're doing shoes at home, arrange to collect shoes on a Saturday morning and return them in the late afternoon. That way you can just do it all at once. If you've got a place to work at a mall on Saturday, collect all your neighborhood customers' shoes on Sunday afternoon and return them in the evening.

Magic shows

You'll do a half-hour routine of magic tricks for kids' parties or community events.

How to start:

Have fliers printed up and distribute them to daycare centers, nursery schools and grade schools.

Pass out fliers at the local mall on Saturdays and around the neighborhood.

Post fliers in community centers, religious centers and local variety stores.

Put an ad in the local paper.

Cost to you:

You'll need a basic magic kit and you'll need to buy or make a top hat and a cape of some sort.

If you don't have a bike or can't get a drive, you may need bus fare to get to some events.

How to price:

Because you have an entertainment skill, you can charge 50 percent more than your usual hourly rate for a show, even if the show is under an hour long.

How to start:

You can't be shy and expect to make money at this kind of business. If you don't like being the center of attention, you shouldn't try this.

Prepare fliers that list all the characters you can be and pass them out in places such as malls, community centers and schools.

Tell all your friends and family members to keep you in mind for their parties or special events, and ask them to make sure they tell all their friends about your services.

Put an ad in the local paper.

Do free shows at senior citizens' centers. One of the audience may have a grandchild with a birthday coming up.

Success Story

My mother was working at a nursery school when I was first learning magic tricks. Whenever the school had a party for the kids, I'd come and do a free magic act for them. It was a good way to practice my act and to find out what the kids liked and didn't like. I also got a lot of jobs performing at little kids' birthday parties because the kids took my fliers home.

You can volunteer to do any character — a clown, a magician, a silly character who reads silly poems — at a nursery school or grade school. The kids may like you and remember the name of your business. When they're having a party, they'll get their parents to hire you! If you can, try to introduce yourself to parents personally, maybe as they pick up their kids.

Tips:

$ If you're any good at making up funny poems, you can add that onto your service and charge extra for them.

$ You can provide candy, presents or balloons with your poems, and charge 50 percent more than what they cost you.

$ Dress up as a character when you do a show on a special occasion. Dress up as a clown, Santa Claus, the Easter bunny, Valentine's Day Cupid or a Saint Patrick's Day leprechaun. You can also hire yourself out to deliver singing telegrams or gifts on special days.

$ Don't forget to carry a supply of your fliers with you to hand out whenever you're performing.

Pet care

This involves grooming and taking care of pets for busy families or for people on vacation.

How to start:

Put the word out among family members and friends that you're available. Ask them to tell their friends.

Have fliers printed up advertising your services, and pass them out around the neighborhood.

Post fliers in the mall, local stores, and the local veterinarian's office. If the vet knows you, try to get him or her to refer customers to you.

Cost to you:

You will have to pay for the fliers.

You will also need some pet grooming products such as brushes, flea powder and shampoo.

How to price:

Charge by the hour for your work. You should charge your hourly rate for the time it takes to walk or feed the animals. For grooming, you should add another 20 percent or so to your hourly rate.

See if you can find regular customers who want you to walk their pet every day after school or at lunch hour. Give them a flat rate each week that's a little less than if you just do it when they're on vacation.

Tips:

- $ When you're offering to feed and walk people's pets, make sure you advertise that you groom pets as well.
- $ Make it clear that you don't just look after dogs and cats: you can look after and feed all kinds of pets, including birds and goldfish.
- $ If your customers are going on vacation, make sure you have a way of contacting them. Or you can get their veterinarian's name, and a note from them to the vet in case their pet gets sick.

Snow clearing

You'll be cleaning and salting or sanding walks and driveways after big storms, as well as keeping them clear of snow all winter.

How to start:

Pass out fliers around the neighborhood.

Post fliers in places such as stores, malls and community centers.

Go door-to-door after a storm and offer your services to clean walkways.

Cost to you:

You'll have to pay to get fliers printed.

You'll need a good snow shovel if you're going to make any money. You can do more jobs in an hour with a snow blower. Borrow one if you can and as soon as you make enough money, buy your own.

You'll need to buy a supply of salt or sand to put down on icy patches.

How to price:

Charge by the job, keeping in mind that you want to make at least your hourly rate for your time. Charge for one hour's work even if it takes you less than that. That way you'll cover the cost of the salt or sand that you supply.

Tips:

$ If people want you to shovel early in the morning before they leave for work, you can charge extra.

$ There are always kids who want to shovel snow in the winter to pick up extra cash, so you have to offer a better service if you're going to make a business out of it. Supply the salt or sand and have a good snow shovel or a snow blower. Clean off the customer's car as an added service. It only takes you a couple of minutes, but it saves the customer the hassle of doing it. They'll remember you next time.

- $ Give regular customers a deal if they promise to hire you all winter. Be sure to get their places cleaned first after a big snow fall.
- $ Get a snow blower and see if you can get a whole neighborhood to hire you.

Regular car care

You'll be washing, waxing and cleaning snow off cars.

How to start:

Spread the word to family members and friends that you're available for car care.

Have fliers printed up advertising your service and distribute them around the neighborhood and at local malls.

Go door-to-door in the spring and ask if people want their cars washed.

Cost to you:

You'll have to pay to have fliers printed up.

You'll need to buy buckets, brushes, detergent, rags, sponges, a chamois, a portable or hand-held vacuum, interior seat cleaner and car wax.

How to price:

Charge your hourly wage to wash and vacuum the car. Charge a minimum of one hour's work, even

if it doesn't take you that long.

To wax the car, charge the cost of washing the car plus three dollars. This means that if a wash is five dollars, you'll charge eight dollars for a wax.

Offer customers a bit of a discount if they'll hire you to wash and wax their cars on a regular basis.

Tips:

$ Go to the local mall on Saturday and put your fliers on the windshields of the cars in the lot.

$ A good sales pitch doesn't hurt in this business. Point out how much better a washing and waxing job you do than an automatic car wash does — and you don't scratch the paint! Plus, you go directly to their homes.

Lawn care

You will offer to mow, edge, rake and weed lawns.

How to start:

Put out fliers in the neighborhood and at malls and variety stores.

Canvass your family and friends to see if any of them want you to care for their lawns.

Put up fliers at places such as community centers and religious centers.

Go door-to-door in the spring offering to hire yourself out to rake leaves and then convince your customers to hire you to do their lawns all summer.

Cost to you:

You'll have to pay the cost of having fliers printed.

You'll need a good power or gas mower with a grass catcher to save raking time, a lawn edger, garbage bags to bag the grass and a rake. If you

can't borrow these tools from your family, see if you can rent them until you can afford to buy your own.

How to price:

To mow and edge the lawn, charge a couple of dollars over the minimum wage with a one hour minimum fee. Charge the same rate to weed the garden and to rake the leaves or grass.

Give customers a discount if they promise to hire you all summer.

Tips:

$ Take a broom along with you and sweep the walk after you're finished your lawn work.

Customers really appreciate it, and it only takes you a few minutes.

$ If you don't have equipment, try to borrow it from a friend or neighbor. Promise to do their lawn free if you can use their mower for your other jobs.

Photography

You'll be taking photos at special events, doing family or kids' portraits or making home videos of special events.

How to start:

Make sure you know how to use a camera very well. Otherwise people won't pay you for your work. Ask someone who is a good photographer to teach you or take a course in photography.

Pass the word around to friends, family members and neighbors that you're available.

Have fliers printed and distribute them around the neighborhood, local malls, community centers and religious centers.

Offer to take free pictures at charity events, events at local religious centers or family parties. Only charge for the cost of the film or video tape and developing the film. People will be able to see that you do a good job and they'll remember you when they have an event coming up that they want photographed.

Cost to you:

You'll have to pay to have fliers printed up.

You'll need good basic camera equipment and either film or videotape. You'll also have to pay to get the film or videotape developed.

You'll likely have to pay for courses or books on photography.

You may have to pay for bus fare to get to the customer.

How to price:

Charge by the hour. Also charge for the cost of having film or video tapes developed, and add 15 percent onto that price.

Tips:

$ Take photographs of events at senior citizens' centers, local office parties or birthday parties of neighbors or relatives, and send free prints to the individuals. Attach a note or a flier to the pictures that advertises that you're available for hire.

$ If your photos will appear in print, remember to ask them to print a photo credit. (For instance, "Photo by Larry Adler, Rent-A-Kid").

Typing or word processing

This involves typing essays, letters and other documents for people who can't type or don't have time to type.

How to start:

You must have access to a good typewriter or a computer that has a good printer. You also have to be able to type accurately and at a fairly fast rate if you're going to make any money.

Put the word out among family and friends that you're available for typing.

Type up a flier (to show how accurate you are), and have it printed. Pass the fliers around the neighborhood and the local mall and drop some off to small businesses in the area.

Advertise a student rate on fliers you put up at high schools, universities and colleges.

Cost to you:

You'll have to pay to have fliers printed or print them on a computer printer.

You'll need a good typewriter or computer. If your family doesn't have one, you may want to rent a machine by the month or lease one to buy. With the money you make in your typing business, you can pay it off in a fairly short time. (Make sure you have enough business lined up to pay for the rental

Success Story

When I first started mowing lawns, that was all I thought I could do. But as I was doing it, I saw other gardening work that I was sure I could do, so I offered to do it. Eventually, I started listing these services on my fliers and offered full gardening care.

When autumn came, I got work digging gardens and pulling plants. That was usually when I'd offer to clear my customers' walks in the winter. Eventually, Rent-A-Kid had year-round customers for yard work.

Just because you start with one kind of thing doesn't mean you can't keep adding. For instance, if you're baby-sitting for a family, see if they want you to make bag lunches for their kids as well, and add that service to your list. Or, if you're cleaning out someone's garage, you can offer to help them with a yard sale, too. Then, if one business slows down, the others are there to keep you going.

If you look around and keep your eyes open, there's always a chance to add services and expand your business!

before you sign a contract!)

You'll need paper and ribbons, and you may want to buy a good dictionary to check your spelling.

You'll have to pay for bus fare if you're picking up or delivering the typing work.

How to price:

Figure out how many pages you can type in an hour. Add 50 percent to your usual hourly rate, and divide it by the number of pages you can type in an hour. Charge this amount per page, even if your customer supplies the paper. (Check other typing services, too, to see if your rates are competitive).

Charge 25 percent extra if the customer wants you to correct spelling errors. Charge extra if there are a lot of numbers or a lot of columns to be typed.

Charge another 10 or 15 dollars if you pick up and deliver the work, and charge 25 percent more if it's a rush job.

Tips:

$ Offer students a discount of five cents a page and they'll tell all their friends about you.

6

Selling Your Own Products: Turning a Hobby into Cash

There are times when a hobby can provide you with a business you didn't even realize was possible. For instance, if you're good at sewing, growing flowers, making kites or painting pictures, you could be sitting on a gold mine.

If you have a creative talent, *make it work for you!*

These businesses also require some investment for materials or supplies to get you going. Many of them, though, will pay back your initial investment (the money you put into them), in no time.

> **TIP:** In this chapter we talk about charging a standard hourly rate for your work. If you haven't decided on your rate, see page 33 for tips on figuring out what to charge.

Selling greeting cards

This involves designing, making and selling your own greeting cards.

How to get your product:

Design original cards for special occasions such as birthdays, Christmas, anniversaries, Hanukkah and weddings. You can even make birth announcement cards and get-well cards. All-occasion (blank) cards also sell well. Make several of each kind to show to customers as samples.

Use simple designs or cartoons and bright colors. Write simple messages or jokes in them. Make sure you design the cards to fit in regular-sized envelopes.

If you have a computer, figure out how to design your cards with it. Make up ten similar cards and package them with ten envelopes to sell as a set.

How to start:

Put samples of each kind of card in a folder. Go door-to-door showing the cards and taking orders.

Ask managers of local card stores and gift stores if they will buy your cards to sell to customers.

Have fliers printed up with drawings of sample cards and pass them out in the neighborhood, malls and community centers.

Cost to you:

You'll have to pay to have fliers printed.

You'll need to buy paper, envelopes and art supplies.

You'll have to buy a display folder for showing your samples and some small paper or plastic bags to hold your sets of cards.

How to price:

Figure out the cost of materials to make ten cards. Figure out how much time it takes you to make ten cards. Then calculate how much you would charge for that time at your hourly rate, and add 50 percent. Add the cost of materials to the cost of your time, and that's your price for a set of cards. Check the going rate to be sure your price is realistic.

For one personalized card, charge that amount divided by five.

Tips:

> $ Once you get orders in for regular cards, start encouraging your customers to order personalized cards for special occasions.

> $ Never copy other greeting cards. It's illegal to copy and sell cards under copyright. Besides, one of the reasons your cards are special is because they are original.

> $ Custom designed cards cost more — point out to customers that they're unique and special.

Selling garden produce

You'll be growing and selling your own fruit, vegetables and flowers during the summer and fall.

How to get your product:

If you're good at gardening, ask if you can have some room in the family garden in the spring. Plant fruits and vegetables such as tomatoes, cucumbers, peas, beans, corn, watermelons and pumpkins, or a variety of flowers.

If you don't know a lot about gardening, ask an experienced adult to give you advice. You can also find a lot of library books to get you started.

Water, weed and fertilize your garden, and when you've picked the produce or flowers, sell them around the neighborhood or to small local stores.

How to start:

Make up fliers and send them around the neighborhood.

Put the word out to family and friends that you grow the best produce in town and sell it at a reasonable price.

Put up fliers advertising your fruit, vegetables or flowers in places such as community centers.

Put your fresh flowers and produce in baskets, load them on a cart or wagon, and take them door-to-door around supper time.

Leave a permanent sign up on your lawn, porch, or balcony to advertise your business so people will stop by to pick things up on their way home.

Cost to you:

You will have to pay to have your fliers printed up.

If you don't live in a house with a yard, or you have no garden space, you could rent space from someone who does. Offer to pay them a percentage of what you make or give them free produce.

You will have to pay for seeds, fertilizer, and weed killer.

You may also have to buy boxes or bags to package your stuff and a wagon or cart if you don't have one.

How to price:

Find out what the local stores and markets are charging for the same thing, and then add a little more to get your price. Advertise in your fliers and when you go door-to-door that, unlike most supermarkets, you deliver and your produce is hand picked and garden fresh.

Sell by the bag or box and offer a discount if people buy two or three items instead of just one.

Tips:

$ If you have a lot of customers and not enough produce, you could find other gardeners in the neighborhood that may have extra vegetables or fruit. Ask them if you can have the extras to sell door-to-door and offer to pay them a percentage of what you earn.

$ You may want to concentrate on selling just one thing. You'll only have to tend one type of plant and they'll all be ready to be picked at the same time. If you plant a crop like pumpkins, you can sell them at two special times, Halloween and Thanksgiving.

Making kids' lunches

This business involves making, packing and delivering kids' school lunches.

How to get your product:

Check the library and go through your family cookbooks and magazines to see what kind of lunch recipes you can find that will make good bag lunches for school. Then think up some interesting, nutritious things to have in the lunches. Make up enough menus so that you can offer a choice of two kinds of lunches for each school day, such as a meat sandwich, fruit and cookies, or a vegetable pita pocket, yogurt and banana bread.

Save up or borrow enough money to buy a couple of weeks' worth of groceries until your customers start paying.

How to start:

Have fliers printed with your logo and sample menus. Pass them out around the neighborhood.

Don't advertise too far from home unless you have someone to drive you around to make deliveries.

Put fliers or notices up in places such as supermarkets and community centers.

Try to get regular orders to make lunches five times a week. Deliver the lunches the night before or early in the morning before the kids leave for school.

Cost to you:

You'll have to pay to have fliers printed up.

You'll have to buy food and the lunch bags.

You may need a wagon or cart for deliveries if your business catches on in the neighborhood.

How to price:

Figure out the cost of ingredients for a week's lunches, and add 10 percent to that cost. Figure out how much shopping, preparing and delivery time a week's lunches will take you, and charge your hourly rate for your hours.

Add your ingredients cost and the cost of your time, and divide by the number of lunches you will be making. That's your price per lunch

Check out what the school cafeterias and local burger joints charge for an average meal. Your prices should be equal or a bit less expensive.

Tips:

$ Make up a logo with the name of your business and put it on the paper you write your menus on. Put your logo on the paper bags that you put the lunches in.

$ Play up the fact that you make fresh, nutritious lunches that kids will like. Point out that your lunches are better for the customers' kids than fast food or cafeteria food.

$ Put a joke or riddle in each bag as a special surprise. If kids love their lunches, they'll ask their parents to keep buying them from you.

$ Some lunch items (for example, cold drinks) cost less if you buy them in bigger quantities. Just make sure you don't buy too much of foods that will spoil.

$ Really take some time and come up with good ideas for food. Also make sure you give a variety of choices. If you do it right, you can promote your business as a gourmet lunch business and get it to the point where kids will think it's cool to carry one of your lunch bags to school.

Selling gift baskets

You'll make and sell specialty gift baskets for special occasions.

How to get your products:

Buy a bunch of small straw or plastic baskets. Decide on a dozen or so different kinds of gift occasions, such as birthdays, anniversaries, baby showers and Valentine's Day.

Decide on three or four items that can go into each different basket, such as toys, candies, balloons, dried flowers, toiletries or ceramic ornaments. Buy enough items to make up six sample baskets to show customers and store owners. Cover the baskets with colored cellophane or plastic wrap, and tie each one with a ribbon.

How to start:

Go door-to-door with sample baskets and ask people to place orders.

Have fliers made up with a list of the kinds of baskets available. Be sure to advertise that you make personalized baskets as well.

Ask managers of local toy and gift stores if they will buy your baskets to sell to their customers.

Cost to you:

You will have to pay to have fliers printed.

You will need to buy the baskets and all the stuff to make your samples.

You may need to buy a wagon or a cart to make deliveries.

How to price:

First figure out your materials cost for 10 average baskets: what it costs for the baskets, the decoration, and the contents. Then add 10 percent.

Figure out how much time it takes you to shop, make up, and deliver ten baskets. Use your standard hourly rate. Combine the cost for materials and the cost of your time, and divide by ten. That's your price per basket.

Charge 50 percent more for personalized baskets.

Tips:

$ If people want personalized baskets, ask for half the price as a deposit so you can buy the extra supplies you'll need.

$ Come up with some original basket ideas, such as a Florida vacation basket with sun tan oil, an inflatable beach ball and a pair of sun glasses, or a "new baby" basket with baby oil, talcum powder, a plastic rattle and a set of ear plugs for the parents.

Setting up a lemonade stand

This business involves selling lemonade and snacks around the neighborhood during the summer.

How to get your product:

Practically every kid in the world has had a lemonade stand on a street corner or on the front lawn. You have to be more creative if you want to make any money at it.

Make a roving lemonade stand by setting up your lemonade stand in a wagon or sturdy cart.

Your drink has to taste really good if people are going to come back for seconds. Buy lemonade crystals and frozen lemonade or fresh lemons. Follow the directions to make up the crystals, then add a couple of spoonfuls of frozen lemonade or squeeze in the juice and some pulp from fresh lemons. Experiment until your lemonade tastes great!

Bake or buy simple cookies or pretzels to sell with the lemonade. Get a couple of big insulated thermos bottles to keep the lemonade cool and add lots of ice.

How to start:

Put big colorful signs on your wagon stating the price of your lemonade and snacks. Wander the neighborhood so people can see you. Also, put signs around the neighborhood saying when and where you'll be sitting still for a couple of hours a day.

Watch for people working in their yards, and go to local business and sell to the workers on their breaks. If you make a habit of going to these places about the same time every day, you'll soon have regular customers who will be waiting for you.

Cost to you:

If you decide to advertise with fliers, you'll have to pay to have them printed.

You'll need to buy a wagon or cart.

You'll need to buy thermos bottles, cups, snacks, paper napkins and garbage bags, plus the lemonade fixings.

How to price:

Figure out how many snacks there are in a package, and divide the cost of the package by that number. That's what each snack costs you. Charge double that price to your customers.

Your lemonade should cost about five cents less than a can of soda pop at the corner store. If, for example, it costs you twenty cents to make a glass of lemonade and a can of pop costs fifty cents at the store, you raise the price of your lemonade to forty-five cents a glass. With a profit of twenty-five cents a glass, you'll make back the cost of your investment in no time.

To figure out what it costs you to make each batch of lemonade, figure out how many cups and napkins you use with each batch of lemonade and how much they cost you. Then calculate how many cups of lemonade you get from each batch. Divide the cost by that number, and that's what it costs you per glass.

Tips:
- $ Make up a batch of low-calorie lemonade as well as your regular lemonade. Make sure your sign says you sell both kinds. That way you can sell to people who are dieting.
- $ On the weekends, take your roving lemonade stand through the local parks two or three times a day and call out, as if you were selling popcorn and peanuts at a baseball game!

Making custom-designed T-shirts

You'll be custom designing, making and selling T-shirts.

How to get your product:

Buy T-shirts in a couple of colors and in small, medium, and large sizes. Buy iron-ons, glitter paint and permanent markers and create some wild designs on T-shirts to use as samples.

Decorate shirts with pictures, patterns, sayings

or your own cartoons. Fold them to show the decoration and put them in plastic bags to protect them.

How to start:

Distribute advertising fliers in the neighborhood and in local schools, the library, malls, and other suitable places.

Go door-to-door with T-shirt samples and take customer orders.

Go to local baseball, soccer and hockey games, and show your samples. Encourage the players to order custom-made team shirts.

Show your samples to managers of clothing and gift stores and see if they'll buy them to sell to their customers.

Cost to you:

You'll have to pay to have fliers printed.

Most of your cost will be in buying shirts for samples and the supplies to design them.

When you're making a custom-designed shirt, you should get at least half the price of the shirt as a deposit from the customer.

How to price:

Figure out the cost of making up ten T-shirts and add the amount of time it took to do them at your hourly rate. Divide by ten and double the price.

Tips:

> $ Stress the fact that your shirts are custom-made and that customers can order any design they want.
>
> $ Give discounts to groups or teams who buy a lot of the same kind of T-shirt.
>
> $ For large orders you might want to get your design screen-printed professionally onto T-shirts. You might earn a little less, but it can save you a lot of time and frustration.

Selling crafts

This business involves making and selling specialty crafts and seasonal decorations.

How to get your product:

Pick a couple of things you're really good at making, such as kites, plant hangers, scented candles, wall plaques, Christmas decorations, dried flower centerpieces or wooden bird feeders.

Save or borrow the money you need to make up a bunch of samples of your products. Make the samples and then package them nicely so they'll be attractive to customers.

How to start:

Make up fliers advertising your products and

send them out around the neighborhood. Put them up in variety stores and community centers.

Advertise in the local paper.

Display your samples at the local flea market or craft fair and take orders.

Spread the word around to friends and relatives that you're in the craft business.

Cost to you:

You'll have to pay for fliers.

You'll need to buy materials or supplies to make and package your crafts.

How to price:

Figure out what it costs to buy the materials to make your product and add 15 percent. Then figure out the cost of your time at your hourly rate and add 50 percent to that. Add those two numbers, and that's your price for the product.

Tips:

$ If your product is a copy of someone else's, it isn't going to stand out in a crowd. It may also be against the law. Make your major selling point the fact that each of your products is handmade and each is a little different.

Making baby or doll clothes

This business involves designing and making baby clothes or doll clothes.

How to get your product:

Find or invent simple patterns for a few outfits. Make the outfits in a couple of different sizes and colors.

Package your samples in plastic or cellophane.

How to start:

Have fliers printed to advertise your business and pass them out around the neighborhood.

Spread the word to family and friends that

you're in the business of making clothes.

Put up notices at locations such as schools, religious centers and community centers.

Hand out fliers at any local children's events, such as fairs or parties.

Show managers or owners of local baby or toy stores your samples and offer to sell them your product.

Cost to you:

You'll need to pay to have fliers printed.

You'll have to pay for sewing materials and some nice packaging materials, and for any patterns you don't create yourself.

How to price:

Figure out how much materials cost for an item, and add 25 percent to the total. Then figure out how much time it takes you to make each piece, and calculate your time at your hourly rate. Add the two totals together to arrive at a price for an item.

Tips:

$ Stress that each piece is a handmade original. Get or make some little labels that advertise that the product is handmade by you, and sew a label in each piece to make it look more professional.

TIP: When you're trying to sell a product, you have to make sure people know they're getting something special at a good price. So take the time to package your product so it looks good. People love brand names and labels, and they'll go back and buy the same ones over and over. Design some kind of flashy logo for your business and order a rubber stamp of it. Then make sure it's on everything that you use — fliers, bills, receipts, boxes and bags. *Keep using your logo and soon people will start to recognize it and associate it with your business.*

Customizing scarves and mittens

You'll be embroidering and decorating mittens and scarves.

How to get your product:

Find a good supply of inexpensive, plain mittens and scarves at a discount store. Buy embroidery wool, beads, sequins and fabric paint at a craft store. Take the scarves and mittens and decorate them — around the cuffs and on the back of the mittens, and on the ends of the scarves. Remember, it doesn't always take a lot of decorating to make something look special. If you take custom orders, you could embroider names or initials on the mittens.

How to start:

Have fliers printed up to advertise your products and pass them out around the neighborhood, malls, and community centers.

Put the word out among family and friends that you're making and selling sets of scarves and mittens.

Show samples to owners and managers of clothing and gift stores and ask if they'll order some to sell to their customers.

Cost to you:

You'll have to pay to have fliers printed up.

You'll have to buy the scarves and mittens, and the wool and beads for decorating, as well as cellophane for packaging.

How to price:

Figure out the cost of your materials for one set, and add 15 percent. Figure out how much time it takes you to make a set and multiply by your hourly rate. Add the materials cost and the cost of your time together, and that's your price per set.

Tips:

$ Give people a discount if they buy more than one set of scarves and mittens at a time.

$ Encourage people to order sets in the colors they like best, and charge a little extra to customize the sets with initials or special trimming. Point out that busy parents can keep their kids' mitts from getting lost!

Making kitchen magnets

This involves designing and making personalized magnets to hold messages on refrigerator doors.

How to get your product:

Buy small plain magnets from a craft or hardware store.

Buy or make small shapes to glue to the magnets, and paint the magnets with faces, sayings, pictures or patterns.

Prepare some magnets as samples to show customers.

How to start:

Take samples door-to-door and advertise that you'll custom-design magnets for birthdays and other special occasions.

Pass out fliers in the neighborhood, at local malls, to small businesses and to any business that caters to tourists.

Go to stores and try to drum up orders by convincing the store managers and owners that a great promotion idea is to give customers free magnets painted with the name of the store.

Get tourist outlets to order magnets custompainted with the name of the town or the tourist site.

Cost to you:

You'll have to pay to have fliers printed up.

You'll have to pay for materials and art supplies to make samples.

How to price:

Figure out the cost of the materials to make a dozen magnets, and add 15 percent. Figure out how much time it takes you to make a dozen magnets, and calculate your time at your hourly rate. Add the two totals together and divide by twelve. That's your price for one magnet.

Tips:

$ Play up the fact that the magnets are inexpensive and a good way for businesses and groups to promote their names.

$ Give discounts to stores or groups that order more than a dozen magnets at a time.

$ You may eventually want to expand your business to making paperweights or notepaper clips.

Selling home baking

You'll be baking and selling goods for special occasions.

How to get your product:

Pick two or three baked goods that you're good at making and experiment with the recipes until you have unique ones.

Using your own recipes, make and package some baked goods and freeze them to use as samples.

How to start:

Have fliers printed up to advertise your baked goods and pass them out around the neighborhood, local malls and the community center.

Go door-to-door with samples of your baking. Leave a flier and an order form with the customers so they'll call you when they need a special dessert.

Spread the word to friends and family members that you're in the home baking business and ask them to buy their next birthday cake from you.

Buy or make up special boxes or bags to package your baking. Put your own logo on everything.

Cost to you:

You'll have to pay to have fliers printed.

You'll have to pay for boxes or bags, and a rubber stamp of your logo to put on them.

How to price:

Figure out the cost of food supplies to make up a batch of your baking. Add 15 percent to that. Then figure out how much time it takes you, and calculate the cost of your time at your hourly rate. Add these two costs to get your price for a batch.

It's a good idea to find out what the local bakery shops charge for similar products and to price your baked goods at similar or slightly lower prices.

Tips:

$ Sara Lee cakes and Pepperidge Farm cookies are really good products that are well-packaged and sold at a medium high price. Put some time and a little bit of energy into snappy packaging for your baked products.

$ Volunteer to donate some baking to community events or parties at senior citizen centers and pass out your advertising fliers with the food.

7

Set Up for Start Up

Now that you know what business or businesses you're in, you have to set yourself up and start bringing in the customers.

The thing to do next is to find yourself a place from where you can run the business. It doesn't have to take up much room; it can be just a small area where you can keep your papers organized and keep a schedule of jobs or delivery dates.

I found out very quickly that it's important to stay organized. You can end up with lots of little pieces of paper floating around. Here are some tips, things that I learned about keeping myself organized:

✔ Get or make a big calendar or date book and write in all the jobs and appointments you have coming up.

✔ Get a receipt book from an office supply store so you can give receipts to customers.

✔ Get blank paper so you'll have something handy on which to write or type up job agreements, contracts, and invoices or bills. You can use a rubber stamp of your logo to make letterhead paper, or design it on a computer.

✔ Get an address book or index card file for customer addresses and phone numbers.

✔ Get a book in which you can keep a weekly or monthly list of your money coming in (income) and your money going out (expenses).

INCOME/EXPENSE SHEET

Date	Amount in	Who paid	Amount out	Who paid
Weekly totals:				
Balance:				

ORDER FORM

Order form number: _____

Date ordered: _____

Name: _____

Address: _____

Phone number: _____

Date job is to be done: _____

Who is doing job: _____

Amount to be paid: _____

When payment is due: _____

Customer signature: _____

RECEIPT

Receipt number: _____

Date: _____

Received from: _____

Amount: _____

For: _____

Signed: _____

```
┌─────────────────────────────────────────┐
│              INVOICE                     │
│  Invoice number:                         │
│  ─────────────────────────────────────── │
│  Date:                                   │
│  ─────────────────────────────────────── │
│  Job (order number):                     │
│  ─────────────────────────────────────── │
│  Name:                                   │
│  ─────────────────────────────────────── │
│  Address:                                │
│  ─────────────────────────────────────── │
│  Phone number:                           │
│  ─────────────────────────────────────── │
│  Work done:                              │
│  ─────────────────────────────────────── │
│  Work completed:                         │
│  ─────────────────────────────────────── │
│  Amount owing:                           │
│  ─────────────────────────────────────── │
│         Payable upon receipt             │
└─────────────────────────────────────────┘
```

You may not need all this paperwork when you begin your business, and you may never expand enough to need it at all. But if you do expand, you'll be glad you started with it from the very beginning. I found it just helped keep me on top of the work and helped me avoid disasters.

Setting up a bank account

Bank accounts are useful for helping you keep track of the money you make. They also help you save money. There are two basic kinds of accounts — checking and savings.

Usually you can write only one or two free checks a month on a savings account. I didn't get a checking account for the first three years I was in business. I only needed a savings account because I didn't need to pay out much money.

If you start a business making and selling something, you may need a checking account so you can keep track of what you pay for supplies.

Once you've got your paperwork set up and a bank account opened, it's time to do some marketing or promotion to get some customers.

Picking the right promotions

You need customers if your business is going to make money. The way to get them is to advertise your service or product. I think fliers are a great way to advertise. They're cheap, they're easy to distribute, and you can use them to reach a lot of people.

Writing and designing a flier:

✓ Make sure the printing is in big, easy-to-read letters.

✓ Make it clear what it is you are selling.

✓ Make it clear why people should buy from you.

✓ Make sure your name and phone number are easy to see.

✓ Don't give your address or people will tend to drop in and see you at inconvenient times.

✓ Tell customers why they should contact you or, in other words, what's in it for them.

✓ If your price is your big selling point, then make that the biggest point in your flier. If your service is your best asset, say that. If your quality is the big drawing card, make that clear. If convenience, taste, style or reliability are the things you want to point out, make sure you do!

✓ People love coupons. If you're offering a special, put one in!

Put drawings or cartoon characters on your flier or make up a company symbol or logo that will catch the eye.

Use active, punchy words such as *first class, bargains, quality, fast* and *speedy.*

If you have the money and think you will benefit from a newspaper ad, make it up using the same principles and the same kinds of words as you used for your flier. Follow the same guidelines when making notices, signs or banners.

Sales pitches:

Going door-to-door or making phone calls to sell your services can be very productive. Remember to be clear and polite and to tell the customer up front what you want to sell.

The first few seconds are the most important. And tell them what's in it for them. For example, "Hi. My name is Larry. I represent Rent-A-Kid. We do lawns and gardening. If I could mow your lawn for less than you're paying now and edge it free, would you hire me?"

You've told who you are, what you offer and what's in it for them. That's all you have to do. Be pleasant if they say no. The customers may change their minds and call you later, especially if you leave them a flier. Call on them again the next time you're out to see if they've thought about it. Be pleasant, polite and persistent.

If they seem interested but haven't said yes, go on and say something else. Tell them more. For example, "We have very competitive prices, and we do good reliable work. We have a lot of satisfied customers in the neighborhood and they'd be happy to give us a reference. Would you be interested in hiring us to mow your lawn or trim your hedges?"

Creating special promotions:

One of the best ways to get people to try your product or service is to give away "two for one" coupons that give two products for the price of one. For example, your coupon could read: "Two car washes/gift baskets for the price of one. Offer good until the end of (month, year)." Or offer a guarantee. If you can get them to hire you the first time, half the work is done. If you do a good job the customer will hire you again, at full price!

Another good promotion is to give away something that costs less than the product it's paired with. For example, "All this week, get a free five-dollar car wash with every eight-dollar wax job!"

Donating part of your sales' profits to a charity can also bring in customers. For example, "For every pet-care package sold this month, Rent-A-Kid will donate one dollar to the local animal shelter!"

Giving away free introductory offer coupons is a great way to interest people in trying your service or product once. If you're as good as you say you are, they'll come back for your service or product and be happy to pay for it.

Volunteering your service or product for charity events in return for a mention of your name is another good way to start getting customers to think of you. Donate a cake to a school party. Donate free lawn care to a religious center in return for a mention in the weekly bulletin. Do a free clown or magic show at the seniors' center or local daycare center.

The best promotion of all, though, is by word of mouth. People talk to one another. If you do good work or make a good product for a good price, word will get around. Unfortunately, the reverse is also true. If you do bad work and you're unreliable, word gets out about that too.

Your best promotion is your good name!

8
Ready ... Set ... Work!

Now that you've figured out what business or businesses you want to run, how you're going to start and set up, how you're going to get customers and advertise and what you're going to charge, all your planning is done.

It's time to get to work and *make your business a success!*

The verbal contract

When people are phoning you because of your fliers or announcements, or hiring you from your door-to-door visits, there are some basic things you have to agree on.

✓ Find out exactly what the customer wants you to do.

✓ Agree on a reasonable amount of time for you to deliver or complete the work. If a customer wants a rush job, explain that you'll charge 10 percent extra.

✓ Give the customer an estimate of the price, or say you'll call right back as soon as you work out an estimate. If it's a painting or cleaning job, you may want to go and look at what's involved before you give an estimate.

✓ Once you give an estimate, you should charge close to that price, even if the work ends up being worth more. But if the customer hasn't given you all the facts about the job, then you can charge more and explain why. The longer you work and the more experience you get, the more accurate your estimates are going to be.

✓ You and the customer should agree on a price or an estimate for the work *before* you begin the job. Decide together if you will be paid by cash or check and when you will be paid.

✓ Ask for a deposit in advance if the job is a big one that will make you a lot of money and take a lot of time, or if it requires you to put out a lot of money for supplies, such as baking for, or planning a large party.

✓ Get the customer's name, address and phone number.

✓ If you're doing a small job like mowing one lawn, you can do all this verbally. For larger jobs, it's a good idea to write all this down and get a signature from the customer on an order form, such as the example in the previous chapter. That way, everybody knows what's expected.

These things may seem like a lot to do, particularly if you're just mowing a lawn, but it saves you hundreds of problems. If everything is clear at the beginning, there are no problems later on.

Now it's time to figure out the best way for you to do the work. If you have several customers who all want different jobs done at the same time, you may be in trouble before you start. It's sometimes worthwhile to bring in someone to help you with the work to make sure it gets done.

In most cases, especially if it's a one-time thing, you may want to give your friend 40 percent of the money you get. Because you advertised and got the customer, and it's your idea and your business, you get 60 percent.

If you often need to bring in people to help you, you may agree to keep this split, or you may just agree on an hourly rate for your helpers. Figure it out on paper and see which works out better for you.

Good and bad things about having a partner

Good	Bad
They do half the work.	You always have to share the decision-making.
You can do more projects and make more money.	The control of the business is no longer yours alone.
Two heads are better than one	You can get into arguments about how the work is done.

I always wanted control of my business, so I found that, if I needed help and didn't want to let a customer down, it was best for me to bring in a friend on individual jobs at the last minute and split the money 60-40.

Good and bad things about having employees

Good	Bad
You can expand your business into areas you can't handle alone.	You have to supervise the work.
You make the decisions about the business yourself.	You have to look at child labor law, and you may have to get insurance.
You can do more work in less time and make more money.	Kids goof off or don't turn up to do work.

I always called the people I hired "sub-contractors" so I didn't have to pay taxes and have all the hassles of being an employer. This leaves you with less responsibility. You should check with your local chamber of commerce or ask your parents to help find out what your responsibilities are.

I kept a large percentage of the money because I was the one who got the customers, contracted to do the work, did all the paperwork and collected the payment.

Success Story

At the end of my first summer with Rent-A-Kid, I had figured out a way to make more money in a day by hiring someone to split the work with me. I had a bunch of townhouse residents as customers for lawn mowing and it took me about 15 minutes to do each lawn, front and back. That was four in an hour and I made 20 dollars. It would have taken me five hours to do all 20 lawns. I would have made 100 dollars in that time, or 50 dollars in two and a half hours.

I got a friend to work with me. One of us did the front lawn, the other the back. We did 20 lawns in two and a half hours and split the money 60 percent for me and 40 percent for my friend. I made 60 dollars in two and a half hours. That's 10 dollars more than if I'd worked alone for the same amount of time. My friend made 40 dollars in two and a half hours. He wouldn't have made any money otherwise, because he didn't have his own business and regular customers.

This is the kind of thing you start to figure out if you keep your eyes open for ways to improve the way you do your work and run your business.

How to treat your customers

When I was running Rent-A-Kid I was always polite and treated customers with respect, even the few who tried to take advantage of me. I never used bad language and I'm never cocky or smart-mouthed with my customers. I treat them the way I want them to treat me — with respect.

Be friendly and polite but always be businesslike. Don't be casual or assume anything about work you're doing for a friend of the family or a relative. Make sure you discuss and agree on everything right up front, just like you would with any customer. That avoids misunderstandings and arguments when it is time to collect payment.

Don't sell the same product to stores that are across the mall from each other or that are close competitors. Neither store will do as well with the product as if one had it exclusively, and they may not order from you again.

I learned that it's really in your own best interest to keep to yourself any personal stuff you find out about your customers through overhearing a family fight or something like that. You'll get a reputation for being trustworthy, and customers like that a lot.

How to collect your money

You should agree on the amount and time of payment before you begin a job. If regular customers sometimes don't have the money at the moment, you may want to give them a bill. Give them a few days to pay it before you bug them. But it's not a good idea to do that with too many customers. It's better to agree to collect the payment on the same day that the work is completed.

If the customer is a stranger or someone who doesn't use your service regularly, ask for your money as soon as you finish the job or, if they're not around, go back at dinnertime to collect. It's not hard to do. Just ask politely. For example, "Hi. I was over this morning to mow the lawn. Can I have my

Success Story

A couple of times customers didn't pay me on big jobs that were worth a lot of money to me. I typed up bills on Rent-A-Kid letterhead and they read: "This bill is overdue. We tried to contact you several times, but you were not at home. If you do not pay this bill within seven days, we will contact our attorney."

The customers paid.

money now please?" or "Hi. I'm finished the lawn now. Can you please pay me?"

If they say they can't pay you now, say, "Well, I'll come back later today or first thing tomorrow."

Be polite and be persistent. If it takes a customer more than seven days to pay you, tell your parents and ask them to help you collect.

Don't do any more work for people who owe you money unless they have a good reason for not being able to pay, such as being on vacation or in the hospital. Wait until they've paid what they owe. If customers are always late paying you and make it a hassle, you're better off dropping them from your work list.

How to handle problems that are bound to come up

On big jobs, where you're doing a lot of work and expect to make a lot of money, for example painting a house or doing the gardening for an apartment or townhouse complex, it's best to write out a contract and get the customer to sign it. State:

- the work you agree to do
- what the customer agrees to pay you,
- when the job is to be completed
- the method of payment.

That way, you both know the score, and there aren't any problems later on.

If a customer's check bounces, take a copy of it back to the customer and ask for it to be replaced with cash. Also have the customer pay your bank's service charge. Don't assume the customer is wrong. Banks often make mistakes. It's not fair to blame the customer without giving him or her a chance to explain.

Dealing with customer complaints

Sometimes customers aren't satisfied with the work you do or with the product you provide. You may not agree with them, but don't get crabby. Listen to them. Negotiate. Explain why you think they're being unreasonable and try to get a partial payment.

If you just can't agree, say you still don't agree with them and leave. Then ask a parent or advisor for some ideas for helping you get some payment. No matter what the outcome, scratch those customers off your customer list and don't do any more work for them.

Sometimes the customers aren't satisfied and you can admit you haven't done as good a job as you could or the product was faulty. Be polite and pleasant. Apologize and offer to do the work again or supply a new product. The customers will respect you for it, and you'll get more business from them and they may recommend you to other people.

Dealing with the law

If you're trying to set up your own business, it's a good idea to have an older person you trust to advise you. It can be a parent, a teacher, a guidance counselor, a friend of the family, an older brother or sister or anyone who you know will take you seriously and help you figure out what your best move is. You have to remember that you're still a kid and you're just learning. You need help from someone with more experience in life.

One area where you're not going to know much is in the area of laws and taxes. If you make less than a certain amount of money each year, you don't have to file a tax return. But if your business starts to boom, you may have to start paying taxes. Get an adult advisor to help you find out what you need to know. Or call the Internal Revenue Service or Revenue Canada and find out what you have to do.

If you're hiring other kids to work for you, call the labor department and find out who to talk to about labor laws for children. Also speak to someone about what your legal responsibilities are if you hire other kids to help you. Some states and provinces require all kinds of paperwork when you're hiring kids and it may be more trouble than it's worth for you to do it.

Dealing with damages

It's very likely that sometime in your work career you're going to have an accident and break a window or a piece of the customer's equipment. Don't panic and don't try to hide the fact that you did it. Tell the customer what happened. Apologize and offer to pay for anything within reason that was damaged by your negligence or inattention. If the customer's equipment was faulty, explain that and negotiate a settlement.

If you've hired other kids to do work and they break something or mess up, go to the customer, apologize, and offer to make up for any damages. Then go to the kids you hired and ask them to pay you for the damages. If they won't do it, don't hire them again. Always do your best to make up for any damage or mistakes, and try not to make the same ones again.

Working safely

There are some safety rules that every kid who owns a business should follow. Some of them are just common sense, but I think it's important to mention them anyway.

Before you ever touch a piece of equipment, always read its instruction manual. If there isn't a manual available, get an adult who's experienced with the equipment to show you how to use it safely.

Don't treat equipment or machines like toys. They're not to be played with. They must be handled with proper care.

Always tell your parents or guardians where you are going to be and when you expect to be back. If you'll be at two or three different places, leave a list of them on the kitchen table.

Never go inside a stranger's home. Always stay outside the door. If you get work that means going inside a stranger's home, always have your parents or guardian check them out with you first.

If you see an open door or a broken window at a home you're working at or looking after, and you know the owners are away, call the police.

Make sure you have phone numbers for the fire department, the police, ambulance and a family doctor whenever you're baby-sitting. Also make sure you have the number where the parents will be.

Always handle toxic materials such as gas, cleaning fluids, paint and garden chemicals with care. Don't leave them out where little kids or animals can get into them. Store them properly and always make sure they're well sealed.

Never try to do heavy work or lift things that are

beyond your physical strength. Get help from someone.

Wear proper clothing for the work you're doing. Wear protection from the direct sun and wear mittens, boots and other cold-weather gear in the winter. Never do yard work in bare feet.

If you're not sure about a piece of equipment or a situation that may be dangerous, go and get advice from someone who knows how to handle it.

9

The Seven Great
Secrets to Success

When I was starting my business, there wasn't anything like this book about business written for people my age. I guess that's because adults don't believe children are interested. Or maybe they don't believe kids are capable of running a business.

Whatever the reason, I had to find out a lot of things on my own. I asked adults and read business magazines and tried to make the information apply to me. You've already read a lot of that information in earlier chapters of this book.

Still, it's up to you to make a success of your own business. Other people can tell you how to start, but they can't do it for you. Nobody can guarantee success, but there are some things I've learned that can help:

1. Do That Little Bit Extra

Spend that little bit of time needed to finish a job properly. Don't rush and leave a mess behind. Don't take shortcuts that will ruin the quality of your work. It's okay to look for ways to speed up your work or make it more efficient, but not if it means quality suffers.

2. Ask For What You Want

Don't be afraid to call people up and ask them to hire you, to give you a deal or to help you with something. Have the courage to speak up and ask for what you want. If they can't give it to you or they don't want to, all they can do is say no.

3. Believe In Yourself

Have faith in your ability to get where you want to go. Believe that you can deliver any reasonable service or product that you say you can. If people say no to you or if you fall short, don't lose faith in yourself. Try and try again.

4. Hang In And Go For It

When it gets hard or confusing, it's tempting to give up. Don't! Stay at it. If something doesn't work, figure out what went wrong, and do your best to fix it or find another way to do it.

5. Don't Be Afraid Of Mistakes

Everybody makes mistakes, even adults. Don't be afraid of doing something wrong. Successful people probably make more mistakes than others because they take more risks. Lots of people are successful because of their mistakes. Their mistakes forced them to find another way to do things. And don't be afraid to ask questions so you can learn from your mistakes.

6. Don't Take On Too Much

Don't get carried away and take on too much work at once. You'll let some of your customers down and lose their confidence if you say "yes" to too many people.

Your reputation for reliability is more important than anything. It's like money in the bank. Make sure you get one thing organized and running smoothly before you take on a new project.

7. Keep Your Eyes Open

There are always opportunities out there just waiting for you to tune in to them. Pay attention to what you're doing and ask questions, and you'll see how one thing is connected to another. You'll also find that one person knows another person who knows another and you'll have doors opened that you didn't even know were there.

Let go of the things that aren't working for you any more and give yourself time to try new things.

I put a lot of hours into Rent-A-Kid and made a lot of money for a kid in a part-time business. The most important thing I learned in making it work was that what I do best is sell myself.

I'm my best product!

My creativity, my ideas, my willingness to work hard and my drive are my best assets.

I also learned that you have to balance a business life and a regular life. I still work hard at my businesses, but I'm still a regular teenager. I keep my grades up and I still have time to hang out with my friends, work out at the gym, go on dates and take vacations with my family.

I just happened to stumble onto the answer most people spend a lifetime looking for. You've got to keep all the aspects of your life in balance and believe in your own ability to make your life a success.

So, now that you know it can be done, get out there and start your own business!

Dear Reader,

I'd like to know how *YOUR* business does! Write to me at:

Adler Development Corporation

785-F Rockville Pike, Suite 502

Rockville, MD

20852

U.S.A.

Larry

Larry Adler

Glossary

account arrangement you make with a bank to handle your money

accountant professional who records, sorts out and reports on a business's financial matters

advertisement announcement by flier or in the media that promotes your product or service

asset something valuable

attorney person who has legal power to act for another person or company; lawyer

bank place where money is deposited by, kept for and loaned out to customers

bill written statement of money owing for a job done or product puchased; invoice

bounced check check which the bank has returned to you when it could not be cashed; usually because the account on which the check has been written doesn't contain enough money to cover the amount

budget plan for the amount of money you have available, and how to use it

business associate person you work with

business card wallet-sized card printed with your own and your company name

canvass go around asking in person for job orders

cash actual money, in bills and coins; not a check

chamber of commerce committee of leaders and business people who organize the business life of a community

charity organization that works for the good of others

check written permission to your bank to withdraw a certain amount of money to give to another person

checking account account that allows you to write checks, paying little or no interest

classifieds section in newspaper where people advertise things

company a business

consumer potential customer

consultant person who advises a company

contract agreement, either written or verbal, binding you to a deal

copyright laws protecting original writing that prevent it being copied without permission

coupon ticket that entitles a customer to get something in exchange, usually a discount

custom (order or **design)** variation of a product, specially requested by a customer

customer person who buys a product or service

deadline date on which work promised must be done

debt money owed to someone

deposit percentage of the price paid by the customer before the job is done; or money put into a bank account

discount cheaper price than the regular one

employee person you pay to work for you

employer person who has employees

entrepreneur a person who starts his or her own business

equipment tools or machines you need to do a job

estimate statement of how much a job will cost and how long it will take

expenses costs you have to pay in order to run your business and make your products

fee an amount of money

financial having to do with money

financial independence having enough money at hand for all your needs

flat rate set price for a series of jobs, rather than an hourly rate for each one

flier a paper distributed door-to-door advertising your company

fundraiser project to raise money for a charity

going rate the usual amount charged for products or services in your area

guarantee company's promise that their customer will be satisfied with his or her purchase

income money you get through earning a wage or interest from a bank account, or from sales

insurance arrangement for a payment of money in case of an accident

interest percentage a bank pays you for the use of your money, or that you pay for a loan

investment putting time or money into a project

invoice form for showing what services have been done or products purchased and the price of each one

job order a detailed written description of a job

law rules set by government

lawyer professional who advises others about laws, and can act for them in court

lease contract for use of equipment, or store or office space

lease to buy lease that gives you the chance to buy something after your lease on it ends

legal allowed by law

liability legal responsibility

license legal permission, usually written

loan amount of money borrowed from a bank or another person, on which you usually have to pay interest

logo drawing or letter design that represents your company name

manufacturer person or company that makes a product

marketing planning for promotion and sale of a product or service

mark-up the amount you add to your cost to get your selling price, necessary to earn a profit

media (the) newspapers, magazines, radio, television

minimum wage smallest legal amount you can pay an employee

negotiation talking about and arranging a deal

networking developing business connections

ownership having possession of something

partner business associate who owns a part of your business

payable to be paid

percentage part of something, measured out of one hundred

postage the amount of money you pay to mail a letter or package

press release news update a company sends out to inform the media of an event, product or service

product something a company makes and sells

profit amount a company makes from sales after expenses have been paid

promotion way of making yourself and your company known

public relations way of dealing with the public

purchase buy

rebate   a partial refund

receipt   having been received; or a written statement that a product or service has been paid for

reference   a recommendation from someone who knows you personally or knows the good work you do

refund   return to a customer of the price he or she has paid for a product or service

rent   daily, weekly or monthly payment for use of equipment or space

resume   a brief description of a person's education and job history

sales representative   person employed by a company to sell its products

savings account   bank account that pays interest, designed for saving money

service   something a company does for pay

sub-contractor   another company you hire to do part or all of a job you have been hired to do

supervise   look over and direct a job and the people doing it

tax   money paid to government to support its services

trademark   a legally registered logo or company name

trade show   meeting of manufacturers and sellers at which new products are shown and deals are made

withdrawal   money taken from a bank account

word of mouth   when customers tell their friends about your company's products or services

The Authors

Larry Adler started his business empire with $19.00 in savings when he was nine years old. By the time he was 12 he had 25 other kids working for him, and by 14 he was the youngest sales representative in North America, specializing in products for kids. Today Larry is focusing on bringing his philosophy of success through hard work and enthusiasm to other kids.

C. Lee Crawford is a freelance writer and broadcaster who has had articles published in *Canadian Living, TV Guide, Toronto Life* and *The Globe and Mail*, among others. She has also appeared on numerous television shows. In her spare time she is a blues singer with two bands.

Lee lives in Toronto, but spent time in Maryland interviewing and working with her co-author Larry Adler. *Rent-A-Kid* is her third book.